Cedar Crest College Library
Allentown, Pennsylvania

D1235345

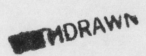

WITHDRAWN

LANGUAGE TYPOLOGY

19th and 20th Century Views

KIBBEY M. HORNE

681770

GEORGETOWN UNIVERSITY PRESS
WASHINGTON, D.C., 20007

Copyright © 1966 by Georgetown University
Printed in the United States of America
Library of Congress Catalog Card Number: 66-21168

CONTENTS

INTRODUCTION

It is unfortunate that for the average student there is very little descriptive literature easily available concerning general theories of language typology. Although a number of typologists, in advancing their own theories, briefly summarize and criticize the work of their predecessors, these summaries are usually more critical than descriptive or merely informative. They are, moreover, often difficult to find, expensive to acquire, largely in German, and not always, for the beginner, clear either in their organization or in their manner of exposition.

This monograph, which represents the first three chapters of my doctoral dissertation at Georgetown University, attempts to summarize the principal nineteenth and twentieth century theories of language typology as their originators presented them. When, however, the understanding of a particular theory seemed to require it, I have added a brief explanation or expansion. The emphasis throughout the survey is on morphological typologies, since historically this has been the primary orientation of attempts at formal classification of language.

I would like to express my appreciation to Professor Kurt Jankowsky of Georgetown University for his advice and assistance in the preparation of the original thesis, and to Professor Hans Krabusch, my tutor and old friend at the University of Heidelberg.

Kibbey M. Horne

1

LANGUAGE CLASSIFICATION

The scientist necessarily attempts to group the subjects of his investigation so that he can make generalizations for the group which will be valid for every one of the group's members. The scientific linguist is no different in this respect from any other scientist--he seeks to reduce the total inventory of languages to a manageable number of homogeneous groupings, which under certain prescribed limitations can be handled as a whole. Attempts at language grouping or classification, therefore, are as old as the systematic study of language itself.

Criteria

Pursuing the scientific intent of language investigation, any attempt at classification must meet certain scientific criteria. As Greenberg points out,[1] such a classification should be non-arbitrary (i.e. the criteria applied should always lead to the same results), exhaustive (i.e. all languages without exception should be classified by the application of the criteria), and unique (i.e. no language should fall into more than one classification). It has, however, been the unfortunate experience of many linguists that such a complex human activity as language does not easily lend itself to scientifically precise classification.

In general, language classification has been approached in four major ways: genetically, areally, sociolinguistically, and typologically. Although by no means a standard usage, the resulting groupings are commonly referred to as genetic families, areal groups, sociolinguistic types, and typological classes.

Genetic approach

The genetic approach, which classifies languages according
to their historical antecedents, is the only one of the four
approaches which meets the three demands of nonarbitrariness,
exhaustiveness, and uniqueness; a fact which gave rise to
Meillet's famous characterization of the genetic approach as
"la seule classification linguistique qui ait une valeur et une
utilité."[2] From a diachronic standpoint this may well be true,
but it does appear to be an overstatement of the method's usefulness. The fact that two or more languages share a common
ancestor in the distant past is always of interest, but in a syn-
chronic study of language this interest may be only academic.
It does not necessarily have anything useful to say about what a
language is, but only about what it once was.
    The genetic approach dominated almost the entire nineteenth
century, when linguists--or perhaps more properly, philologists
--devoted themselves to the diachronic comparison of languages.
The traditional division of Indo-European languages into Indo-
Iranian, Balto-Slavic, Armenian, Albanic, Hellenic, Italic,
Celtic, and Germanic is an example of genetic classification.
In the twentieth century the approach is still almost universally
accepted, the work of Antoine Meillet (1866-1936) being an out-
standing example.

Areal approach

    The areal, or geographic, approach to linguistic classifica-
tion is more concerned with where a language is spoken, rather
than with what it is like. In cases of doubt as to genetic relationship, as for example in the Sudanic languages, an areal
classification can be of real value. Perhaps the best known
example of an areal classification is the linguistic atlas[3] of
Father Wilhelm Schmidt (1868-1954), which shows the geographical distribution of the major language groups. Schmidt's atlas
is also noteworthy in that it shows the geographic distribution not
just of the languages alone but of other language features as well.
At the phonological level he describes the geographical distribution of certain sounds in initial position (three subdivisions) and
in final position (five subdivisions). At the syntactic level he
describes the distribution of different categories of number with
nouns and personal pronouns (nine categories) as well as the use
of inclusive and exclusive 'we'. At the morphological level he

describes the geographical distribution of seven contrasting word groupings in all of their combinations, e.g. 'animate' vs. 'inanimate', 'people' vs. 'things', and 'masculine' vs. 'feminine' vs. 'neuter'. At the lexical level he describes the geographical distribution of counting systems (ten categories). He even attempts a sort of sociolinguistic approach by correlating the position of the genitive (six subdivisions) with the existence of partial or complete matriarchy.

Sociolinguistic approach

More typical of the sociolinguistic approach, however, is the seven-part classification of language[4] proposed by William A. Stewart (1930-), which is based on the relative possession (+) or non-possession (−) of four attributes: historicity (a demonstrable historical development through use), standardization, vitality (possession of native speakers), and homogenicity[5] (whether lexicon and grammar derive from pre-stages of the same language).
Stewart's seven resulting language types, with an example of each, are as follows:

Attributes				Type	Example
Histor-icity	Standard-ization	Vitality	Homogen-icity		
+	+	+	±	Standard	English
+	+	−	+	Classical	Latin
+	−	+	+	Vernacular	Acadian
+	−	+	−	Creole	Krio
+	−	−	−	Pidgin	Neo-Melanesian
−	+	−	±	Artificial	Volapük
−	−	−	±	Marginal	"household languages"

Despite certain shortcomings in economy of description,[6] Stewart's classification has a great range of usefulness in describing language situations, particularly when the language type is coupled with one or more of the seven functions that Stewart discriminates: official, group, wider communication, educational, literary, religious, and technical. Function may well be an inseparable part of Stewart's classification, in that the goal of the sociolinguistic approach is to describe who uses a particular language and for what purpose.

Such a classification is by its very nature non-unique, since different people use the same language for different purposes. Hebrew, for example, was a classical language prior to the establishment of post-World War II Israel, where it is now a standard language; while in the United States, Hebrew remains a classical language, used for religious purposes. Standardization may vary between countries as well: the German of Germany is relatively standard but that of Switzerland is not, in which latter country its type is more that of a vernacular.

Typological approach

The fourth approach to language classification, the typological, treats language so to speak in isolation, without regard to history, location, or social role. Since this approach deals only with the observable phenomena of language and groups languages according to the presence or absence of these phenomena, the typological approach should be the most scientific of all four approaches and theoretically should be capable of being accomplished with scientific exactitude. In practice, however, the results to date have been disappointing and often frustrating.

In large part the source of the disappointment and frustration in achieving a satisfactory typology appears to lie in the complexity of language itself, i.e. in the embarrassingly rich inventory of observable phenomena. As a result one finds a variety of typologies for almost every level of language organization (phonological, morphological, syntactic, and semantic) and for the areas where levels overlap or the line of demarcation is obscure (canonic, suprasegmental, and symbolic). Lexicon alone seems never to have been advanced seriously as a basis for a typology, due no doubt to the difficulties of establishing a meaningful grouping of languages whose only common bond is the possession or lack of certain words.

Phonological typologies

Phonological typologies may range in complexity from a single-sound classification such as the click languages, or a simple dichotomy like the satem vs. centum classification of Indo-European languages, to an elaborate arrangement of distinctive features along the lines laid down by Jakobson, Fant, and Halle.[7] A forerunner in phonological typology was Nikolas S.

Trubetzkoy (1890-1938), who concerned himself with typing vocalic systems in 1929[8] (the main distinction being between triangular, as in Spanish, and quadrangular, as in Finnish, vowel patterns) and with consonantal systems in 1931.[9] Charles F. Hockett proposed an extensive phonological typology in 1955,[10] and in recent years C. F. Voegelin (1906-   ) has led a number of workers in this field.[11]

It is also possible to classify languages according to their canonic form, that is, in terms of how consonants (C) and vowels (V) are combined to give a grammatical unit. Old Church Slavic and Japanese, for example, could be classified as typically open-syllable languages, with a further subdivision into consonant clustering (sestra 'sister') and non-consonant-clustering (mimashitaraba 'had I seen') respectively. Pursuing the thought of clustering, English (splurged /CCCVCCC/) and German (spritzt /CCCVCCC/) have pronounced consonant clusters, but require the presence of a vowel, which Czech for one does not (prst 'finger' /CCCC/). This might provide an additional category. It would also be desirable to establish some gauge as to the degree of consonant clustering, since the Slavic languages tend to go much farther in this regard than, say, the Germanic; e.g. Russian /vzglat/ 'glance' and /vdobstf/ 'comforts'. No unified theory of language classification according to canonic form has been advanced, but many writers including Greenberg[12] and Martinet[13] have remarked on its possibilities.

Morphological typologies

The next level in the linguistic hierarchy comprises the morphological typologies, which will be treated later in detail. In general, however, it can be said that traditionally linguists have been more concerned with classifications based on morphological processes than with any other system of classification except genetic. There was a strong conviction among most nineteenth century Indo-European linguists that the word was the basic building block of language, and much of their attention was necessarily devoted to the morphological aspect of structure. But more of this later.

Suprasegmental typologies

Somewhere between morphology and syntax falls a classification based on the suprasegmental, or prosodic, features of intonation, tone, and accent. Intonation is apparently too subject to variation to provide any promising basis for a typology, but tone and accent do offer possibilities.

For tone, Martinet[14] offers a possible five point scale:

(1) has tones or not, e.g. Swedish vs. English;

(2) has tone on all intonable segments or only some, e.g. Ibo vs. Lithuanian;

(3) tone is punctual or melodic, e.g. Japanese vs. Danish;

(4) tone, if melodic, is on same or different registers, e.g. Mandarin Chinese vs. Vietnamese;

(5) tone may be applied to syllable, e.g. Serbo-Croatian; segment smaller than a syllable, or mora, e.g. languages of Central Africa; or segment larger than a syllable, e.g. Norwegian.

Indicative of the difficulties of typologizing, Greenberg[15] offers a four point scale to classify the same languages from the standpoint of tone: nontonal, having level tones, having contour tones, or having both level and contour tones.

As for accent, i.e. stress, pitch, or length, Martinet[16] offers another five-way classification, this time according to whether the language:

(1) is accented or not, e.g. English vs. Vietnamese;

(2) has an unpredictable or predictable place of accent, e.g. Spanish vs. Polish;

(3) is limited or unlimited in the distribution of the place of accent, e.g. Spanish vs. Russian;

(4) if tone exists only under accent, has two, three, or some other number of tone distinctions, e.g. Swedish 2 vs. Latvian 3;

(5) is word-accenting or lexeme-accenting, e.g. Russian vs. German.

Syntactic typologies

Syntactic classifications are relatively uncommon, but capable of almost infinite variation. Martinet[17] again offers an example, based on the dichotomy between languages in which all lexical morphemes perform the same basic functions (e.g. where 'leg' and 'it walks' are identical) and languages in which some verbal morphemes are restricted exclusively to predicative use (e.g. where '(it) walks' can only be a predicate). Languages with a verbal class can be further subdivided into those in which non-verbal lexemes can normally be used with predicative function (as in Russian) and those in which this is formally impossible (as in English). [18] One can readily imagine typologies based on other divisions: according to the possession of personal verbs (French) or only impersonal verbs (Tibetan); having nouns of two genders (Spanish), three genders (German), or none (English); according to multiple divisions of tense or case, or other similar devices.

Lexical typologies

As stated earlier, lexical typologies have never been advanced seriously. In general terms, however, one could speak of the relative motivation, or productivity, of languages; that is, the degree to which the lexicon of different languages can be expanded by composition or derivation. By such a method, German could be classified as a language with a very productive lexicon, while French would stand as relatively unproductive, or "arbitrary". Such a discrimination is vague at best, however, if one wishes to classify all of the languages of the world.

Semantic typologies

Semantic classification offers a system that appears more useful to the scholar. If one accepts, even in part, the Sapir-Whorf hypothesis that man interprets the world as his language presents it to him, [19] then it might be possible to select a semantic classification of language in such a manner that it might be correlated directly with a significant anthropological phenomenon. Numbering systems, for example, might be the basis for such a division, particularly among primitive peoples.

Symbolic typologies

Last of the typological possibilities is the suggestion advanced by Greenberg[20] that it may be possible to derive a symbolic typology, i.e. one which involves sound and meaning simultaneously. As an example of such a typology, Greenberg offers those languages in which a nasal consonant is always employed in the word for 'mother'. This would appear to be a capricious typology at best, and at worst one which would fly in the face of the accepted principle of the arbitrariness of speech sounds.

Ethnocentric theories

One point that will not be dealt with at length here is the
speculation that languages inexorably and in response to some
natural law evolve from one class to another. Most nineteenth
century linguists[21] were convinced that language began as a
crude, haphazard means of communication; developed through
more complex and somehow finer and more aesthetically
pleasing stages; to flower eventually in that most noble of language groups, the one to which the native language of the inves-
tigator belonged.

Despite historical evidence to the contrary, this supposed
evolution was for Schleicher and other nineteenth century linguists a movement from the simple, or isolating, to the complex,
or flexional,[22] languages. The twentieth century has seen the
continuation of this type of theory, where linguistic evolution has
even been made the handmaiden of political development as seen
through Marxist eyes. N. J. Marr (1864-1934),[23] for example,
expounded the "stadialistic" theory: that an amorphous linguistic
structure existed at the time when primitive peoples allegedly
lived in a sort of Proto-Communism; and as society developed a
more highly stratified division of labor, its language became
correspondingly more complex, i.e. agglutinative. The cul-
mination of this process was for Marr a class-society with a
technical division of labor and with a highly complex, i.e.
flexional, language. In order to claim superiority both for
Communism as the supposed original state of society and for
Russian as an example of the final stage of linguistic development, Marr in his later works developed the theme that this
linguistic development is not the result of a historical increase
in complexity, but actually is the uncovering of elements which
existed in the distant past. One of the somewhat startling results
of this reverse logic is that Marr is thus able to claim that
French is typologically older than Latin.

Much of the disrepute into which linguistic typology has fallen
is traceable to unfortunate ethnocentric theories of this type.
However, it is not the purpose of this study to criticize these
theories in detail, as they have been amply discussed elsewhere.[24]

NOTES

1 Joseph H. Greenberg, Essays in Linguistics (Chicago: University of Chicago Press, 1957), p. 66.
2 Antoine Meillet, "Introduction à la Classification des Langues," Linguistique Historique et Linguistique Générale (Paris: Champion, 1948), appendix, pp. 53-69.
3 Wilhelm Schmidt, Die Sprachfamilien und Sprachenkreise der Erde (Heidelberg: Carl Winters Universitäts buch-handlung, 1926).
4 William A. Stewart, "An Outline of Linguistic Typology for Describing Multilingualism," Study of the Role of Second Languages in Asia, Africa, and Latin America (Washington: Center for Applied Linguistics of the Modern Language Association of America, 1962), pp. 15-25.
5 In later lectures, Stewart has used the word "zygosity" to express the same thought.
6 It is interesting to note that from a classificatory point of view the attribute of homogenicity serves only to differentiate creole and vernacular, and is otherwise a redundant and ambivalent criterion. Similarly, historicity exists as a somewhat vague criterion created solely to show the sudden, artificial appearance of a manufactured language instead of the gradual development of a natural language. The system would profit from a third, more discriminating criterion in lieu of homogenicity and historicity.
7 Roman Jakobson, C. Gunnar M. Fant, and Morris Halle, Preliminaries to Speech Analysis: The Distinctive Features and Their Correlates (Cambridge: The MIT Press, 1961).
8 Nikolas S. Trubetzkoy, "Zur allgemeinen Theorie der phonologischen Vokalsysteme," Travaux du Cercle Linguistique de Prague, I (1929), pp. 39-67.
9 Nikolas S. Trubetzkoy, "Die phonologischen Systeme," Travaux du Cercle Linguistique de Prague, IV (1931), pp. 96-116.
10 Charles F. Hockett, "A Manual of Phonology," International Journal of American Linguistics, XXI, No. 4 (1955).
11 C. F. Voegelin, "Methods for Typologizing Directly and by Distinctive Features (in reference to Uto-Aztecan and Kiowa-Tanoan vowel systems)," Lingua, XI (1962), pp. 469-487, is one example.
12 Joseph H. Greenberg, "The Nature and Uses of Linguistic Typologies," International Journal of American Linguistics,

XXIII, No. 2 (1957), p. 71.

13 André Martinet, A Functional View of Language (Oxford: Oxford University Press, 1962), pp. 75-76.

14 Ibid., pp. 84-85. The examples are mine.

15 Greenberg, IJAL, XXIII, No. 2, 74.

16 Martinet, A Functional View ..., 85-86. Again the examples are mine.

17 Ibid., pp. 100-101.

18 Martinet overstates his case. I knife him, he legged it up the street, and hand it over all employ nonverbal English lexemes with predicative function. There are many other examples in English.

19 Benjamin Lee Whorf, "Linguistics as an Exact Science," Collected Papers on Metalinguistics (Washington: Foreign Service Institute, 1952), p. 11. See also Whorf, "Science and Linguistics," ibid., p. 5.

20 Greenberg, IJAL, XXIII, No. 2, 71.

21 Wilhelm von Humboldt was a notable exception.

22 Confusion often arises between the current use of "inflec-tional" (as opposed to "derivational") to describe relational morphemes, and "inflectional" to describe those languages which employ flexion or internal modification of the root. For that reason in this paper "inflection", "inflective", and "inflectional" as they apply in the second sense will be replaced where possible by "flexion" and "flexional". Spelling with an x will indicate in every case that internal modification of the root is meant.
It might also be noted here that, unless the source document is identified as a translation, all translations from German into English are my own. Placing the German word in parentheses after the English translation indicates that this was the word used in the German original.

23 See Lawrence L. Thomas, The Linguistic Theories of N. Ja. Marr ("University of California Publications in Lin-guistics," Vol. XIV; Berkeley: University of California Press, 1957).

24 For a brief survey of linguistic evolutionary theory, see Joseph H. Greenberg, Essays in Linguistics (Chicago: University of Chicago Press, 1957), pp. 56-65.

2

THE NINETEENTH CENTURY

1 EARLY THEORIES (1808-1850)

If modern comparative linguistics can be said to date from
the speech of Sir William Jones (1746-1794) before the Asiatic
Society on February 2, 1786, formal attempts at systematic language typology were begun a scant twenty-two years later.

Friedrich von Schlegel

It was in 1808 that Friedrich von Schlegel (1772-1829) published Ueber die Sprache und Weisheit der Indier in which he
established two classes of languages:
    Either modifications of meaning are indicated by internal
    change of the root-sound, by flexion; or ... by a separate
    added word which taken by itself means plural, past, a
    future obligation, or other relational concepts of a similar
    nature; and these two simple situations characterize the
    two main classes of all language. [1]
Schlegel's division of Sprachen durch Flexion and Sprachen
durch Affixa is easily exemplified. [2] The German blieb
'remained' shows an internal change or flexion to the root
bleib-; while the Turkish kaldi 'remained' shows an unchanged
root kal-, to which affixes have been added to show preterite
and third person singular. The fact that German also has
parallel affixing constructions such as stell-te 'placed', or
mixed flexional-affixing constructions such as brann-te 'burned'

(from brenn-) does not in itself make German an affixing language. The fact that German is capable of inner flexion to an
appreciable but not necessarily total degree is the test of its
being a flexional language.[3]

It is important to bear in mind that Schlegel conceived of
affixation as an extremely broad term, which embraces all
gradations of affinity between the root and the elements added to
it to give some secondary modification in meaning. Thus Chinese,
where the added element is a separable word which is completely
independent of the root, is still an affixing language in the Schle-
gelian scheme of things, although at the very bottom of the scale.
Amerindian, Basque, and Coptic despite the complexity of their
structure are also affixing languages, but at the upper end of the
scale; for their affixed elements "fuse and coalesce to a certain
degree with the root."[4] As a result there is, as Jespersen has
noted,[5] the germ of a third division in Schlegel's two-part
scheme. Languages can be considered as flexional or non-
flexional, in which latter case they may be subdivided into affixing (in the current sense of the word) or nonaffixing.

August von Schlegel

Friedrich's brother, August Wilhelm von Schlegel (1767-1845),
formalized this three-way classification in 1818,[6] when he
divided languages into:
    (1) languages without any grammatical structure;
    (2) languages which employ affixes;
    (3) languages with inflexion.
The first class is exemplified by Chinese and is characterized
by having roots which are incapable of development or modification. Syntax, or the relationship between words in the sentence,
consists for the languages of this class in placing these inflexible
elements of language next to each other. The distinctive character of the second class of languages, on the other hand, is that
they express secondary ideas and relationships by attaching
elements to other words. The third class, languages with inflexion, is marked by the modification of "letters", i.e. sounds,[7]
of the roots and by addition to the roots of derivative syllables.

Like his brother before him, August von Schlegel finds[8] that
all of the indigenous American languages, as reported by
Alexander von Humboldt in the description of his Voyage aux
régions equinoxials du nouveau continent, seem to be affixing.
August von Schlegel also mentions Humboldt's paper on Basque,

a language which he feels to be "equally characterized by affixes."[9]

August von Schlegel does add an additional classificatory tool by further subdividing flexional languages into two subclasses, synthetic and analytic:

Languages with inflexion are divided into two types, which I will call synthetic languages and analytic languages. I mean by analytic languages those which are obliged to use an article before nouns, personal pronouns before verbs, which resort to auxiliary verbs in conjugation, which make up by prepositions those case endings which they lack, which express comparative degrees of adjectives by adverbs, and so forth. The synthetic languages are those which dispense with all these means of circumlocution.

For Schlegel this subdivision serves largely to differentiate the classical languages and their modern successors. Greek, Latin, and Sanskrit are held to be synthetic, in that they express the relationship of one word to another by the forms of the words themselves, e.g. Latin casa virī 'the man's house'. The Romance languages, on the other hand, are analytic in that they express these same relationships by means of other words and by word position, e.g. Spanish la casa del hombre 'the man's house'. The Germanic languages are thought by Schlegel[11] to form an intermediate class, since they are synthetic in origin but tend strongly to analytic forms, e.g. English the man's house or the house of the man.

Wilhelm von Humboldt

It remained for Wilhelm von Humboldt (1767-1835) to add a fourth class and to establish the morphological typology that would dominate the linguistic scene for the next one hundred years. Humboldt's classification was first published in 1822 in a lecture to the Akademie der Wissenschaften in Berlin, entitled Ueber das Entstehen der grammatischen Formen, und ihren Einfluss auf die Ideenentwicklung[12] and was expanded greatly from 1830 to 1835 in Ueber die Verschiedenheit des menschlichen Sprachbaues und ihren Einfluss auf die geistige Entwicklung des Menschengeschlechts,[13] which was the introduction to the three volumes of Ueber die Kawisprache auf der Insel Java, published between 1836 and 1840. In Humboldt's classification "besides Chinese, which dispenses with all grammatical forms, [there are] three

possible forms of language: the flexional, agglutinative, and incorporating."[14] Since earlier in his work[15] Humboldt mentions
Chinese in connection with the isolation of words, Humboldt's
classification is usually given as: (1) isolating, (2) flexional,
(3) agglutinative, and (4) incorporating.

Between the lack of all word categories, as in the "grammarless" Chinese, and true flexion or inner root change, Humboldt
finds the only conceivable possibility to be an "intended but incomplete flexion, a more or less mechanical affixing, not a
truly organic development." [16] This process Humboldt calls
"agglutination," a term which he apparently was the first to use.

Also original with Humboldt is the addition of a fourth class
of language, the incorporating (einverleibend). Characteristic of
incorporation is the fact that affixes are used to indicate what in
other languages would be separate forms, dependent on a verbal
predicate. Instead, the incorporating languages combine in a
single word a verb, subject, object, and various modifiers. Incorporating languages, then as now, are exemplified by the
Amerindian languages, as in the Yana word bulsidibalm?gu?asinza
'I stay three nights' (literally, "three-night-stay-a little-past/
present-I").

Where others, such as the Schlegels, found incorporating languages to be merely an advanced stage of affixation, Humboldt
places them in a separate class due to the nature of the processes
involved. Agglutination he considers to be merely "mechanical
affixing." Flexion is true organic development, but is also inseparable from existence of the word as a unit and of the
sentence as a number of these separate units.[17] Therefore,
where the word is also a sentence, a different type of morphological structure is involved. This different structure he calls incorporation.

Humboldt rejects August von Schlegel's subdivision of inflexional languages as analytic or synthetic. The argument he
employs[18] is that synthesis is supposed to indicate a fusion of
different parts into a single entity, and therefore synthesis pre-
supposes a plurality which is combined. Humboldt cannot find
such a plurality in a form like the German band 'bound' (from
bind-), but only a change in sound. Further, this inner fusion of
two or more parts can be distinguished only partially. One can
never say that fusion is present or absent; to some extent fusion
is always there. To employ the same example, band 'bound', how
can one identify the presence or absence of 'third person singular',
when the same form can also be 'first person singular'--while

first and third persons in the present tense are clearly identified
in the forms bind-e and bind-et respectively?

A second objection to Schlegel's subdivision raised by
Humboldt is that, in the so called analytic languages, there is no
breakdown of all synthetic forms. Rather, only some forms are
replaced by combinations of words, while others are left unchanged. This incomplete breakdown is not confined to the
Germanic languages, which Schlegel characterized as intermediate, but is found in most other languages, such as Persian.
The division between analytic and synthetic, Humboldt feels, is
too unclear for the distinction to be useful.

Franz Bopp

Humboldt's quadripartite classification was not accepted by
all. Franz Bopp (1791-1867) returned in 1833 to a tripartite
classification, in which he carefully avoided both the terms
flexion and agglutination, and instead based his classes on root
forms:[19]

(1) languages with monosyllabic roots, without the capability
of composition and hence without organism, without grammar,
e.g. Chinese;

(2) languages with roots[20] capable of composition and acquiring
their grammar almost exclusively in this manner, e.g. the Indo-
European languages and all others not in classes (1) or (3);

(3) languages with disyllabic roots and three necessary consonants as sole bearers of the meaning of the word, e.g. the
Semitic languages.

For the languages of the second class, the main principle of
word formation under Bopp's scheme is the connection of verbal
and pronominal roots, e.g. German geh-t 'he goes'. For the
third class, grammatical forms are created by composition as
well as inner modification of the roots, e.g. Arabic kataba 'he
writes', from the root ktb.

August Pott

In 1848 August Friedrich Pott (1802-1887) reaffirmed the
typology of Humboldt,[21] dividing language into isolating (Chinese,
Indo-Chinese), agglutinating (Tatar, Turkish, Finnish), flexional
(Indo-European), and incorporating (Amerindian). Pott gives the
classification an added complexity,[22] however, in that he considers the quality of being flexional as the normal condition of

language. Isolating and agglutinating languages are therefore "infranormal"; and incorporating languages are "transnormal" in that they have gone beyond mere flexion. No other linguist seems to have pursued this classification.

August Schleicher

August Schleicher (1821-1868), in addition to advancing the Stammbaum theory of genetic classification, also proposed distributing languages according to their morphological structure. Since Schleicher was under heavy Hegelian influence for much of his lifetime, this morphological classification, first advanced in 1848,[23] and later expanded materially in 1850[24] and 1861-1862,[25] was a tripartite one.

Schleicher proceeds from the assumption that language has meaning (Bedeutung) and relation (Beziehung) and postulates that all languages may be classified as to the manner in which sound is used to express these two elements:[26]

(1) In the monosyllabic (einsylbig) languages, meaning is the only thing indicated by sound; while relation is not overtly expressed, but only suggested by word position.

(2) In the agglutinative (agglutinirend or anleimend) languages, relation is expressed phonologically and affixed loosely to the unchanged meaning-sound.

(3) In the flexional (flectirend) languages, meaning and relation are both expressed by sound, but in such a manner as to be fused into a single word.

Schleicher does not accept Humboldt's assignment of incorporating languages to a fourth and separate class, but considers them to be agglutinative in nature, since both involve only the collection (lose Anfügung) of words.[27] As a further refinement, however, Schleicher applies August von Schlegel's subdivision of synthetic and analytic not only to flexional languages, but to agglutinative ones as well. The criterion applied is the relative degree to which the separate word parts fuse: a close relation being synthetic, a relatively loose relation being analytic.[28]

In a subsequent expansion of his typology,[29] Schleicher introduces the following algebraic notation to clarify the morphological processes involved in each class of language:

R   - root
+ r - juxtaposition of a second, separate root which then
       stands in a known relationship to R

s   - suffix
p   - prefix
i   - infix
x   - (superscript) regular variation

form part of the
word and express
relation, not
meaning

Applying this notation to the classes of language, the following
typology results:

(1) monosyllabic languages, "which are simply composed of
invariable disjointed meaning-sounds,"[30] e.g. Chinese, Annamite, Siamese, and Burmese. Formula: R or R + r;

(2) agglutinative languages, "which can link to these invariable
sounds sounds of relation,"[31] e.g. Finnish, Tatar, Basque,
Amerindian, Bantu, and, for that matter, most languages. These
can be subdivided further into:

(a) synthetic   Rs   Finno-Ugric
                Ri   Tush[32]
                pR
(b) analytic   Rs + r   Tibetan
                pR + r

(3) flexional languages, "which for the purpose of expressing
relation can regularly vary their roots as well as their affixes,"[33]
e.g. Semitic and Indo-European. Flexional languages can be subdivided further into:

(a) synthetic R^x Semitic
                pR^x
                $R^x s^x$ Greek, Latin
(b) analytic $R^x s^x + r$ French, German

It should be noted that the regular use of the prefix ge- in the
German past participle does not indicate the presence of
Schleicher's prefix (p) as shown for Semitic, for the same reason
that Schleicher advances for the Greek augment; namely, that it
"is no relation-affix, no prefix, but an adherent, though originally
independent word."[34] An example of a true pR^x is Arabic jaktubu
'he writes' vs. taktubu 'she writes'.

2 ELABORATIONS (1850-1900)

Heymann Steinthal

Where Bopp had approached language classification according
to the structure of roots, Heymann Steinthal (1823-1899) devised

a structural classification which depends upon the different types
of affixing and of inner flexion. Steinthal's classification first
appeared in 1850,[35] and then in a second and revised edition in
1860.[36]

A key principle for Steinthal's typology is that he considers
"form" to mean not morphology, but syntax, that is, the relationship between words. Thus Chinese, which for other typologists
is "grammarless" or "formless" due to the invariant nature of
its roots, is a form language for Steinthal, since grammatical
relationships are expressed by the collocation (Nebensetzen) of
discrete words. Indo-Chinese, however, is formless for
Steinthal, since its grammatical relationships are not expressed
directly by the collocated elements, but must be deduced there-
from. Incorporating languages, whose sentence-words stand
alone, are similarly formless.

The distinction between "formless" and "form" languages in
Steinthal's classification becomes even more tenuous among the
suffixing languages. Steinthal calls the languages of the Ural-
Altaic family "formless," because their suffixes do not express
relationships between words, but are entities in themselves. The
Indo-European languages, on the other hand, have "real" (i.e.
varying) suffixes which show genuine relationships.

A second key principle in Steinthal's typology is the distinction
between collocating (nebensetzend) and derivative (abwandelnd)
constructions. In general, the distinction is an easy one: invariable
words are collocating, i.e. they can only be placed together me-
chanically; all other words are derivative. This results in the
following classification:[37]

A. Formless languages
  (1) collocating   Indo-Chinese
  (2) derivative
      (a) by reduplication and prefixes   Polynesian
      (b) by suffixes   Turkish
      (c) by incorporation   Amerindian

B. Form languages
  (1) collocating   Chinese
  (2) derivative
      (a) by juxtaposition of   Egyptian
          grammatical elements
      (b) by inner root change   Semitic
      (c) by "real" suffixes   Sanskrit

Max Müller

In 1880 F. Max Müller (1823-1900) returned to Bopp's pre-
occupation with roots as the basis for typology. Reasoning that
all languages can be reduced to predicative and demonstrative
roots, Müller posited three different kinds of languages, depending on how roots are put together.[38]

(1) Roots may be used as words, each root preserving its full
independence. Müller calls this class, which others call monosyllabic or isolating, the "radical stage," and gives as an example Ancient Chinese.

(2) Two roots may be joined together to form a word, and in
the resulting compound one root may lose its independence.
Müller calls this the "terminational stage" instead of agglutinative,
and gives as an example the Turanian[39] languages.

(3) Two roots may be joined together to form a word, and in
the resulting compound both roots may lose their independence.
Müller calls this the "inflectional stage" and gives as an example
the Aryan and Semitic languages.

Müller rejects[40] as unnecessary the possibility of incorporating
(or to use Müller's term, "polysynthetic") languages constituting
a separate class. As long as the "significative" root remains
distinct, the language is agglutinative in nature; as soon as the
root is absorbed, the language may be classified as inflexional.
The relative presence of "phonetic corruption"[41] can, in fact, be
used to distinguish each stage, or class, of language:

(1) The radical stage has no phonetic corruption.

(2) The terminational stage has no phonetic corruption in the
primary root, but may have some in the secondary or determina-
tive elements.

(3) The inflectional stage has phonetic corruption in both its
principal root and in its terminations.

Müller also denies[42] that it is necessary to distinguish synthetic
and analytic subdivisions, since both are flexional in nature, the
first simply representing an earlier historical stage than the
second.

Franz Misteli

Franz Misteli revised Heymann Steinthal's typology in 1893.[43]
Of particular significance in Misteli's revision is the redefinition
of "form," so that to all intents and purposes "form" and "formless" correspond exactly to the "organic" and "inorganic" of

Friedrich von Schlegel. The chief criteria to be applied to morphological classification are (1) the relation of the word to the
sentence, with the verb as the core of the sentence; and (2) the
structure of the word itself.

Only the flexional languages have form under Misteli's definition, since only here are the elements that make up the word
completely fused. The verb is a separate entity at the core of
the sentence, and contains the essential root plus an affix that
indicates the subject. The incorporating languages, on the other
hand, do not distinguish the word from the sentence and therefore
cannot be said to have form. Equally formless are the agglutinative languages which have only "apparent" words, since the
supposed change of their roots is only the addition of other elements and not an internal mutation; and likewise the isolating languages, which have no "words" at all, since their roots cannot
change.

These latter "nonword" languages (nichtwortige Sprachen) are
further subdivided into root-isolating, i.e. having no word-form-
ing affixes of any kind; stem-isolating, i.e. expressing the relationship of one word to other words in the sentence, not in the
structure of the word itself, but by means of affixes which are
not complete words in themselves; and lastly juxtaposing,[44] i.e.
expressing relationships by means of affixes which are complete
words in themselves, but which in combination represent new and
different grammatical categories. The distinction between the two
latter categories is not always clear, but might be clarified somewhat by the following examples: Malay lajar 'sail' (noun) and
belajar 'sail' (verb) show stem-isolation, i.e. an invariant stem
to which an affix is added to show a grammatical relationship.
The Tibetan mamagcañ, literally 'man-head-have' or 'having the
head of a man', shows juxtaposition, i.e. the bringing together of
invariant roots in a single word to express a different grammatical
relationship. Compare these two with an agglutinative construction such as Turkish vil-m 'of the year', where the affix -m indicates a particular relationship which can be applied to any
number of roots, always stating the same relationship.

Misteli's classification then establishes two main groups of
six language classes, which are further divided into four sub-
groups:

    A. Formless languages
        (1) with sentence-words (Ein-Wort-Sätze)   Amerindian

(2) without words (<u>nichtwortig</u>)
    (a) root-isolating   Chinese
    (b) stem-isolating   Malay
    (c) juxtaposing (<u>anreihend</u>)   Egyptian
(3) with apparent words (<u>scheinwortig</u>) Turkish
B. Form languages
    (4) with real words (<u>echtwortig</u>)   Semitic and
                                      Indo-European

F. F. Fortunatov

The last of the six language classes distinguished by Misteli shows that his division does not avoid including within a single language class both the Semitic languages and the highly dis- similar Indo-European languages. This is traditionally a prob- lem and is a difficulty common to all of the typologies advanced thus far, except for those of Bopp and Steinthal. One possible solution to the difficulty was put forward in 1900 by Filipp Fjodorovič Fortunatov (1848-1914), who added a fifth class to Humboldt's traditional four. Fortunatov called his fifth class "flexional agglutinative"[45] - and used it to designate the Semitic languages, in which the root normally consists of three consonants to which varying numbers of vowels are added.

NOTES

1 Friedrich von Schlegel, <u>Ueber die Sprache und Weisheit der Indier</u> (Heidelberg: Mohr und Zimmer, 1808), p. 45. The German text reads:"Entweder werden die Nebenbestimmungen der Bedeutung durch innre Veränderung des Wurzellauts angezeigt, durch Flexion; oder aber jedesmal durch ein eignes hinzugefügtes Wort, was schon an und für sich Mehrheit, Vergangenheit, ein zukünftiges Sollen oder andre Verhältnisbegriffe der Art bedeutet; und diese beiden einfachsten Fälle bezeichnen auch die beiden Hauptgattungen aller Sprache."

2 The example is mine.

3 It is unfortunate that Schlegel's most descriptive writing is directed towards a value judgment of flexional languages as the product of "organic" growth, while affixing languages are said to have roots which are likened "not to fertile seed, but to a heap of atoms which the winds of chance blow together or

apart" (Ueber die Sprache ..., p. 51). This vivid simile has
led many writers to emphasize the organic-inorganic division
rather than the durch Flexion-durch Affixa classification
Schlegel himself uses (ibid., pp. 54-55 ff).

4 Friedrich von Schlegel, ibid., p. 49.
5 Otto Jespersen, Language: Its Nature, Development and
   Origin (New York: Henry Holt and Company, 1922; reprinted
   1925), p. 36.
6 August Wilhelm von Schlegel, Observations sur la langue et
   la littérature provençales (Paris: Librairie grecque-latine-
   allemande, 1818), pp. 14-15.
7 A distinction between letters and sounds was not made by
   Schlegel, or for that matter by Grimm or Humboldt. Rask,
   on the other hand, did make the distinction.
8 Ibid., p. 85, footnote 7.
9 The Voyage is an account of a trip up the Orinoco in 1799 by
   Wilhelm von Humboldt's brother, Alexander. It was, however, Wilhelm who wrote on Basque.
10 August Wilhelm von Schlegel, Observations ..., 8. The
   French text reads: "Les langues à inflexions se subdivisent
   en deux genres, qui j'appellerai les langues synthétiques et
   les langues analytiques. J'entends par langues analytiques
   celles qui sont astreintes à l'emploi de l'article devant les
   substantifs, des pronoms personnels devant les verbes, qui
   ont recours aux verbes auxiliaires dans la conjugaison, qui
   suppléent par des prépositions aux désinences des cas qui
   leur manquent, qui expriment les degrés de comparaison des
   adjectifs par des adverbes, et ainsi du reste. Les langues
   synthétiques sont celles qui se passent de tous ces moyens
   de circonlocution."
11 Ibid., p. 17.
12 Wilhelm von Humboldt, "Ueber das Entstehen der grammatischen Formen, und ihren Einfluss auf die Ideentwicklung,"
   Wilhelm von Humboldt: Werke, ed. Andreas Flitner and
   Klaus Giel (Stuttgart: J. G. Cotta'sche Buchhandlung, 1963),
   III, pp. 31-63.
13 Wilhelm von Humboldt, "Ueber die Verschiedenheit des
   menschlichen Sprachbaues und ihren Einfluss auf die geistige
   Entwicklung des Menschengeschlechts," ibid., III, pp. 368-
   756.
14 Ibid., III, p. 653.
15 Ibid., III, p. 489.
16 Ibid., III, p. 498.

17 Ibid., III, p. 501.
18 Ibid., III, pp. 317-318.
19 Franz Bopp, A Comparative Grammar of the Sanskrit, Zend, Greek, Latin, Lithuanian, Gothic, German, and Sclavonic Languages, trans. Edward B. Eastwick (3rd ed.; London: Williams and Norgate, 1862), I, pp. 102-103.
20 Bopp's classification is complicated by his concept of all Indo-European roots as being monosyllabic. His second class actually states "languages with monosyllabic roots." For the purposes of exhaustiveness of the classification, I have omitted the word "monosyllabic."
21 In Jahrbücher der freien deutschen Akademie, 1. Heft, 1848, cited by Heymann Steinthal, Characteristik der hauptsächlichsten Typen des Sprachbaues (Berlin: Dümmler, 1860), p. 10.
22 Cited by Otto Jespersen, Language, p. 698.
23 August Schleicher, Zur vergleichenden Sprachengeschichte (Bonn: H. B. König, 1848).
24 August Schleicher, Die Sprachen Europas in systematischer Uebersicht (Bonn: H. B. König, 1850).
25 August Schleicher, A Compendium of the Comparative Grammar of the Indo-European, Sanskrit, Greek and Latin Languages, trans. Herbert Bendall (London: Trübner and Company, 1874).
26 August Schleicher, Die Sprachen ..., pp. 7-9. The spelling of the German terms is as used by Schleicher, but is now archaic.
27 August Schleicher, Zur vergleichenden Sprachengeschichte, pp. 9-10, footnote.
28 August Schleicher, Die Sprachen ..., pp. 8-10.
29 August Schleicher, A Compendium ..., pp. 2-3.
30 Ibid., p. 2.
31 Ibid., pp. 2-3.
32 One of the languages of the Caucasus.
33 August Schleicher, Die Sprachen ..., p. 3.
34 Ibid., p. 3, footnote 2.
35 Heymann Steinthal, Die Classifikation der Sprachen, dargestellt als die Entwicklung der Sprachidee (Berlin: Dümmler, 1850).
36 Heymann Steinthal, Characteristik der hauptsächlichsten Typen des Sprachbaues (Berlin: Dümmler, 1860).
37 Ibid., p. 327.
38 F. Max Müller, Lectures on the Science of Language (6th ed.; London: Longmans, Green, and Co., 1880), I, pp. 330-331.

39 The designation "Turanian" applies to agglutinative languages
    as a "family" and includes all American, Asian, and European
    languages which are not Aryan, Semitic, or Chinese. The
    term is not now in general use.
40 Ibid., p. 371.
41 Ibid., p. 372.
42 Ibid., p. 371.
43 Franz Misteli, Characteristik der hauptsächlichsten Typen
    des Sprachbaues (Berlin, 1893), cited by Otto Jespersen,
    Language, pp. 79-80; and by P. S. Kuznecov, Die morphol-
    ogische Klassifikation der Sprachen, trans. K. A. Paffen
    (Halle: VEB Max Niemeyer Verlag, 1960), pp. 13-14.
44 Jespersen on pp. 79-80 of Language translates anreihend as
    "affixing."
45 Cited by P. S. Kuznecov, Die morphologische Klassifikation
    ..., p. 14.

3

THE TWENTIETH CENTURY

1 CONTINUATION OF OLDER VIEWS (1901-1920)

The first two decades of the twentieth century saw no real departure from the traditional typologies of the nineteenth century.

F. N. Finck

Franz Nikolaus Finck (1867-1910) essayed classification from a slightly different standpoint, but the net result of his language classes was a scheme that closely paralleled previous efforts. The distinctions employed by Finck were based on an analysis of two factors: the conceptual complexity of the word, and the "fragmentary character" of its structure. Finck then[1] posited a scale in which Chinese, as a conceptually simple language, i.e. each word being but a single morpheme, represents the approximate center. At the two extremes of the scale lie Greenland Eskimo, whose words are "massive"[2] structures composed of a number of concepts closely connected to a central theme; and Subiya, one of the Bantu languages, whose words are "fragmentary" structures composed of a number of different, only loosely related parts. The other languages arrange themselves about the center, inclining towards one or the other extreme.[3]

Finck is concerned not only with how many concepts are united in a single word, but also with the manner in which they are united. Finck draws the same distinction between root-isolating and stem-isolating as Misteli does, but extends the distinction to the inflexional languages as well. This results in separate classifications for root-inflected and stem-inflected languages. Root-inflected languages are those whose roots remain invariant but which at

the same time show internal flexion. These conditions automat-
ically confine the class membership to the Semitic languages,
which have an invariant root, generally of three consonants, e.g.
the Hebrew root zkr 'remember' to which changing vowels are
added internally and externally. This process is not analogous
to the case of German, where the root contains both vowels and
consonants, one or both of which may show flexion, e.g. singen
vs. sangen and bringen vs. brachten. German, Greek, and
other languages of similar morphological structure are termed
stem-inflected. By this distinction Finck thus divides the Semitic
and Indo-European languages, as did Fortunatov.[4]

Finck goes one step further in adding a third class for those
inflexional languages which often prove troublesome in other
typologies, particularly those typologies which do not distinguish
clearly between morphological and syntactic considerations.
Characteristic of this class, which includes languages such as
Basque and Georgian, is an interdependence of the parts of the
sentence which is expressed in the internal structure of the word.
To use an example from Basque:[5] verb forms depend on the different subject, tense, direct object, and indirect object. Thus
Basque uses 150 forms to express the same meanings as the
three English forms have, has, and had. The Basque word cor-
responding to have in the English phrase I have given the woman
the apple is diot, but the Basque equivalent of have in the phrase
I have given you (plural) the apples is dauzkitzvet. Languages of
this type Finck calls "group-inflected," since they are inflected
for a group of grammatical categories.

Finck's overall classification, first proposed in a study of
German in 1899, was formalized as a book in 1901.[6] Revised in
1909,[7] the classification is as follows:

A. Isolating
    (1) root-isolating   Chinese
    (2) stem-isolating   Samoan
B. Inflected
    (1) root-inflected   Arabic
    (2) stem-inflected   Greek
    (3) group-inflected   Georgian
C. Combining, but not inflected
    (1) juxtaposing (anreihend)   Subiya
    (2) subordinating (unterordnend)   Turkish
    (3) incorporating (einverleibend)   Greenland Eskimo

N. J. Marr

More of historical than of substantive interest are the typological theories of Nikilaj Jakovlevič Marr (1865-1934),[8] who
has already been mentioned for his evolutionary theories along
Marxist lines:

> The primitive, amorphic, synthetic, linguistic structure
> (present in the so-called monosyllabic languages; for exam-
> ple Chinese), the second, agglutinative structure (which
> distinguishes, for example, the Turkish language), and the
> third, flexional structure (which Russian, for example,
> reveals) are not three parallel [types], but three types
> which chronologically follow one another.[9]

Marr's basic division of 1920 is one that does not vary signif-
icantly from that of August von Schlegel, which preceded it by a
hundred years.

2 MODERN THEORIES (1921-1962)

Edward Sapir

The first break with traditional morphological typology came
when Edward Sapir (1884-1939) published his book Language in
1921.[10] Sapir proposed a classification which would provide a
basis for discovering the "intuitional forms"[11] of language,
depending on the interrelation of three sets of distinctions: grammatical concepts, grammatical processes, and firmness of affixation.

The first of these sets of distinctions involves grammatical
concepts, or the relation of one word in the sentence to another.
Sapir distinguishes four classes of such concepts:[12]

I. Basic or concrete concepts, which involve no relations as
such, e.g. farm;

II. Derivational concepts, which give an added or altered
meaning to the root, without involving the rest of the sentence,
e.g. farmer;

III. Concrete relational concepts, which indicate or imply
relations transcending the word to which they are applied, e.g.
farmers;[13]

IV. Pure relational concepts, which are purely abstract and
relate the concrete elements to each other, indicating syntactic

form, e.g. the order in <u>see the farmers</u>, as opposed to <u>the farmers see</u>.

Sapir considers Classes I and IV as being essential to and present in all languages.[14] Classes II and III, on the other hand, exist (in conjunction with I and IV) either separately, together, or not at all. There are then necessarily four major language types according to the manner in which grammatical concepts are expressed:[15]

(A)	I + IV	Simple pure-relational
(B)	I + IV + II	Complex pure-relational
(C)	I + IV + III	Simple mixed-relational
(D)	I + IV + II + III	Complex mixed-relational

This conceptual classification by itself does not take into account the technical aspects of morphological structure, but it does make two important distinctions: It differentiates, first, those languages which keep their roots pure (Types A and C) from those which build up inseparable elements (Types B and D); and, second, those languages which keep their relational concepts free of concrete elements (Types A and B) from those which do not (Types C and D).

The second set of distinctions which Sapir makes addresses itself to these technical aspects, i.e. the grammatical processes.[16] Here Sapir identifies "isolating" languages as those which always identify the word with the root; "affixing" languages as those which affix to the root modifying elements such as prefixes, suffixes, and infixes; and "symbolic", i.e. inflective, languages as those which employ internal modification of vowels and/or consonants, reduplication, or accentual differences of stress and pitch.

Affixing in turn can be further broken down into two processes: "fusing," and "juxtaposing" or "agglutination." Agglutination is considered to be the mechanical juxtaposition of two or more unchanging elements. Fusion, on the other hand, implies more of a "psychological uncertainty"[17] as to where the juncture lies. Thus the construction <u>book-s</u> demonstrates not agglutination, but fusion; for there are other possible plural affixes, such as in <u>ox-en</u>. Where fusion involves no change in the root, it is regular; where the addition of an affix involves a change in the root, it is irregular. In contrast, where there is internal change without affixation, the process is one of symbolism. These differences may be indicated algebraically as:[18]

Type of affixing	Formula	Example
agglutination	$c = a + b$	goodness
regular fusion	$c = a + (b-x) + x$	books
irregular fusion	$c = (a-x) + (b-y) + (x + y)$	depth
symbolism	$c = (a-x) + x$	geese

The subdivision of infixing into two parts results in the following four-way division of grammatical processes:[19] (a) isolating, (b) agglutinative, (c) fusional, (d) symbolic.[20]

This division by itself is of limited value, but when taken in conjunction with the expression of relational concepts, is of much greater usefulness. Each of the four language types, A, B, C and D, which are identified by their manner of expressing grammatical concepts, then may be shown to have subtypes according to the grammatical processes they employ. Significant here is the fact that each of the component groups II, III, and IV of a language type may use a different grammatical process to express relation (Group I of course does not express any relation at all). Arbitrarily granting derivational concepts (II) precedence over relational concepts (III, IV), languages may be identified as "agglutinative-fusional" (IIb, IVc), or "fusional-agglutinative" (IIc, IVb), or the like. A single adjective, such as "agglutinative," indicates that the same process is used for both derivational and relational concepts.

As a process, isolation (a) can only be applied to pure relational concepts (IV), while agglutination (b), fusion (c), and symbolism (d) can be applied to all four classes of concepts. This gives a possibility of 960 language types[21] without using Sapir's device of identifying one type as having a "tinge" of another, or listing the techniques employed in order of their importance.

The third set of distinctions which Sapir applies is based on the "relative firmness with which the affixed elements are united with the core of the word"[22] Sapir recognizes three such degrees of affixation:

(1) analytic: does not combine concepts with single words, e.g. Chinese; or does so sparingly, e.g. English;

(2) synthetic: combines concepts but with restraint, e.g. Latin, Arabic, Finnish;

(3) polysynthetic: combines concepts with extreme elaboration, e.g. Nootka.

Sapir emphasizes[23] that these three terms are purely quantitative and are more useful in defining a tendency towards a certain

Fundamental type	II	III	IV	Technique	Synthesis	Examples
A Simple pure-relational	—	—	a	Isolating	Analytic	Chinese; Annamite
	(d)	—	a, b	Isolating (weakly agglutinative)	Analytic	Ewe (Guinea Coast)
	(b)	—	a, b, c	Agglutinative (mildly agglutinative-fusional)	Analytic	Modern Tibetan
B Complex pure-relational	b, (d)	—	a	Agglutinative-isolating	Analytic	Polynesian
	b	—	a, (b)	Agglutinative-isolating	Polysynthetic	Haida
	c	—	a	Fusional-isolating	Analytic	Cambodgian
	b	—	b	Agglutinative	Synthetic	Turkish
	b, d	(b)	b	Agglutinative (symbolic tinge)	Polysynthetic	Yana (N. California)
	c, d, (b)	—	a, b	Fusional-agglutinative (symbolic tinge)	Synthetic (mildly)	Classical Tibetan
	b	—	c	Agglutinative-fusional	Synthetic (mildly polysynthetic)	Sioux
	c	—	c	Fusional	Synthetic	Salinan (S.W. Calif.)
	d, c	(d)	d, c, a	Symbolic	Analytic	Shilluk (Upper Nile)

				Technique	Degree of Synthesis	Examples
C Simple mixed-relational	(b)	b	—		Synthetic	Bantu
	(c)	c, (d)	a	Fusional	Analytic (mildly synthetic)	French*
D Complex mixed-relational	b, c, d	b	b	Agglutinative (symbolic tinge)	Polysynthetic	Nootka (Vancouver Island)**
	c, (d)	b	—	Fusional-agglutinative	Polysynthetic (mildly)	Chinook (lower Columbia River)
	c, (d)	c, (d), (b)	—	Fusional	Polysynthetic	Algonkin
	c	c, d	a	Fusional	Analytic	English
	c, d	c, d	—	Fusional (symbolic tinge)	Synthetic	Latin, Greek, Sanskrit
	c, b, d	c, d	(a)	Fusional (strongly symbolic)	Synthetic	Takelma (S.W. Oregon)
	d, c	c, d	(a)	Symbolic-fusional	Synthetic	Semitic (Arabic, Hebrew)

* Might nearly as well have come under D.
** Very nearly complex pure-relational.

Reproduced with permission of Harcourt, Brace & World, Inc. from Edward Sapir, Language, pp. 142-143.

type than they are as absolute counters. He further points out[24] that languages of Type A are necessarily analytic; those of Type C are predominantly analytic, sometimes synthetic, but not likely to be polysynthetic; and those of Types B and D can be any one of the three. Applying this third set of distinctions to the first two offers the possibility of 2,640 to 2,870 language types,[25] even without resorting to Sapir's qualifying notations of "mildly," "weakly," or "strongly" before the degree of synthesis. Using all of the possible elaborations and qualifying adverbs, there is the numerical possibility of assigning a separate and distinct language type to every known language.

Thus, by employing three sets of distinctions according to conceptual type, technique, and degree of synthesis, Sapir's system of classification offers a wide variety of possibilities. As an example of the flexibility of the system, Sapir shows a table of twenty-one languages,[26] which is reproduced on pages 30 and 31. The complex possibilities of variation in the scheme represented show a very real break with tradition; for even the most elaborate of previous typologies, such as those of Finck, Steinthal, and Misteli offered only eight language classes. More significant, however, is the manner in which Sapir has changed from the traditional linear approach to a matrix presentation of language features.

Joseph H. Greenberg

The mathematical flavor of modern morphological typology becomes even more pronounced with the proposals of Joseph H. Greenberg (1915-   ), which were read in an unpublished paper in 1949,[27] later published in 1954,[28] and then republished in 1960.[29] Greenberg's method parallels Sapir's proposals in many ways, but sets up five bases instead of Sapir's three (Greenberg's first three bases, as a matter of fact, correspond very closely to Sapir's). The most significant departure in method, however, is Greenberg's definition of each language feature in terms of a ratio of the occurrence of two elements in the same stretch of text, expressed as one of ten numerical indices. These ratios are then interpreted as trends which the language shows, rather than as a single class to which it belongs.

The first basis of classification, or parameter, is "degree of synthesis", indicated by the ratio of morphemes (M) to words (W), or M/W. As an example, the English word sing-ing consists of two morphemes in a single word, and its (1) "index of synthesis" is therefore M/W = 2/1 = 2.0.

The second parameter is "technique" and is expressed as (2) an "index of agglutination", which is the ratio of agglutinative constructions (A) to the number of morph junctures (J), or A/J. These two terms require some explanation. An agglutinative construction is considered to mean each instance in which a morph is added to another morph within the same word, provided both morphs belong to morphemes which are automatic. Thus friend's is an agglutinative construction (A = 1), made up of two automatic morphemes: friend and 's 'possessive'.[30] A morph juncture is found in each instance where two morphs are joined in an agglutinative construction; and there is necessarily one less morph juncture in each word than there are morphs. In friend's, therefore, there is one morph juncture, or J = 1.

The third parameter Greenberg uses is the presence or absence of "derivational and concrete-relational concepts", which are expressed by three indices:

(3) A "compositional index" shows the numbers of roots (R) per word, or R/W.[31] A word like overcoat, for example, is composed of two roots and therefore has a compositional index of R/W = 2/1 = 2.0.

(4) A "derivational index" shows the number of derivational morphemes (D) per word, or D/W. Derivational morphemes are defined by Greenberg as morphemes "which, when in construction with a root morpheme, establish a sequence which may always be substituted for some particular class of single morpheme in all instances without producing a change in the construction."[32] Thus -er in sing-er is a derivational morpheme, since the entire sequence can be replaced by the single morpheme {man} without a change in construction.

(5) A "gross inflectional index" shows the number of inflectional morphemes (I) per word, or I/W. An inflectional morpheme is defined by Greenberg as "a nonroot, nonderivational morpheme."[33] The -s in sing-er-s is a nonderivational morpheme, since any word substituted for the total construction must by polymorphemic, e.g. singers = men = {man} + {plural}.

The fourth parameter is the "order of subordinate elements in relation to the root" and is expressed by two indices:

(6) A "prefixial index" shows the ratio of prefixes (P) to words, or P/W; e.g. pre-judge, P/W = 1/1 = 1.0.

(7) A "suffixial index" shows the ratio of suffixes (S) to words, or S/W; e.g. hate-s, S/W = 1/1 = 1.0.

Infixing, containment (as in Arabic), and intercalation (as in the Semitic languages generally), are considered by Greenberg to be so rare as not to be worth calculating.[34] It is also worth noting that Greenberg considers Sapir's symbolism to fall within this area and to be simply the infixing of an inflective element.[35]

The fifth parameter concerns "devices for relating words to each other" and comprises three indices which are calculated on the basis of the number of nexus (N), a nexus being defined as "each instance of the use of a principle to indicate relations between words in the sentence."[36] This parameter is represented by the following three indices:

(8) An "isolational index" is the ratio of instances of significant order (O) per total nexus, or O/N. The criterion employed is: "absence of an inflectional morpheme in a word was taken as an indication that the method of relating it was order."[37]

(9) A "pure inflectional index" is the ratio of instances of nonconcordial inflectional morphemes (Pi) per total nexus, or Pi/N.

(10) A "concordial index" is the ratio of instances of concordial inflectional morphemes (Co) per total nexus, or Co/N. Where concordial and nonconcordial features are merged in the same inflectional morpheme, the same morpheme is counted a number of times. Thus for Greenberg the -um of Latin masculine singular accusative would be calculated on the basis of Pi = 1 (case) and Co = 2 (gender and number).

The result of this quantitative approach is the calculation of ten indices which, when taken together, give an almost infinitely variable possibility of combinations. Greenberg has calculated the indices for eight representative languages: Sanskrit (Sk) and Anglo-Saxon (AS) as ancient Indo-European languages of the Indo-Iranian and Germanic branches respectively; modern Persian (Per) and English (Eng) as their modern counterparts; Yakut (Yak) as an agglutinative language (instead of Osmanli Turkish which has too many Arabic borrowings); Swahili (Swa) as an agglutinative, concordial Bantu language; Annamite (Ann) as a root-isolating language; and Eskimo (Esk) as a polysynthetic language. The resulting indices are:[38]

		Sk	AS	Per	Eng	Yak	Swa	Ann	Esk
(1)	M/W	2.59	2.12	1.52	1.68	2.17	2.55	1.06	3.72
(2)	A/J	.09	.11	.34	.30	.51	.67	–	.03

(3)	R/W	1.13	1.00	1.03	1.00	1.02	1.00	1.07	1.00
(4)	D/W	.62	.20	.10	.15	.35	.07	.00	1.25
(5)	I/W	.84	.90	.39	.53	.82	.80	.00	1.75
(6)	P/W	.16	.06	.01	.04	.00	1.16	.00	.00
(7)	S/W	1.18	1.03	.49	.64	1.15	.41	.00	2.72
(8)	O/N	.16	.15	.52	.75	.29	.40	1.00	.02
(9)	Pi/N	.46	.47	.29	.14	.59	.19	.00	.46
(10)	Co/N	.38	.38	.19	.11	.12	.41	.00	.38

Greenberg himself finds the synthetic and agglutinative indices to be the most immediately useful in language classification, and proposes the following rule of thumb.[39] A synthetic index of 1.00 to 1.99 indicates an analytic language, 2.00 to 2.99 a synthetic, and any value above 3.00 a polysynthetic language. Similarly, any language with an agglutinative index of over 0.50 may be called agglutinative.

André Martinet

The modern approaches of Sapir and Greenberg have by no means found unanimous acceptance. Representative of the dissenters is André Martinet (1908–   ), who terms Sapir's analysis a "nearly tragic illustration of the pitfalls of psychologism"[40] and dismisses Greenberg's approach as one that "translates Sapir's scheme into currently fashionable jargon."[41]

Martinet does, however, find one original view of Sapir's acceptable: that all languages possess significant units that do not in themselves indicate their relation to the rest of the utterance, e.g. chair; and other units which indicate only what relations the first units have to each other, e.g. with. These two types of units correspond generally to Sapir's Class I and Class IV; but, unlike Sapir, Martinet rejects semantic reference as a principle of linguistic classification and thereby rules out Sapir's intervening classes. He posits instead position as the distinguishing criterion for the two types of units. To Martinet chair has function in an utterance only when it has a given position. The phrase with (the) chair, on the other hand, expresses function regardless of its position.

The first type of indispensable language unit is called by Martinet "lexical" and the second "grammatical." Application of the criterion of whether or not function is indicated yields the following four morphological types:[42]

1 lexical without indication of function chair type	2 grammatical without indication of function the type
3 lexical function indicating yesterday type	4 grammatical function indicating with type

For Martinet this scheme has the merit that it offers a basis for "a typology that transcends formal accidents,"[43] the traditional basis for nongenetic classification of languages. Since the types shown are functional, the same morpheme[44] may belong to several types. From this morphological base, Martinet then derives a grammatical typology,[45] which is based on the possession or nonpossession of exclusively "verbal" morphemes.

Summary

Although it might appear at first glance that the morphological typologies described have very little in common, they are relatively consistent as to which languages should be distinguished from which other languages. To represent graphically this consistency, the chart on pages 40 and 41 shows a side-by-side comparison of the various typologies prior to the classifications of Greenberg and Martinet. While keeping each individual author's scheme of classification intact, the chart attempts to arrange similar classes and similar distinctive features at the same relative horizontal levels. The solid horizontal lines separate major language classes, while the broken horizontal lines separate subclasses (marked by asterisks).

The typologies described, despite their relative consistency regarding what should be distinguished, vary considerably in the manner in which they distinguish between language classes. It is not the purpose of the present survey to examine these differences in detail; but in general it may be said that most of the differences among the typologies discussed can be attributed to one of two factors: (1) the structural level on which a key distinction is made (morphological, syntactic, semantic, or, more rarely, phonological), or (2) the tightness of the psychological bond which individual typologists intuitively judge to exist between the stems and the affixes of particular languages.

The various interpretations of Amerindian languages illus-
trate approaches on different structural levels. These languages
are distinguished as "affixing" on the morphological level, "polysynthetic" on the syntactic level, and "incorporating" on the
semantic level. On the other hand, the relative tightness of the
psychological bond between the elements of a word lies at the
heart of the "affixing-agglutinative-symbolic-fusional terminology.

NOTES

1 Franz Nikolaus Finck, Die Haupttypen des Sprachbaues (3rd
   ed.; Berlin: B. G. Teubner, 1936), p. 150.
2 "Monolithic" might be a better term.
3 Winfred P. Lehmann, Historical Linguistics (New York: Holt,
   Rinehart and Winston, 1963), pp. 53-54, discusses Finck's
   scale as if Chinese lay at the end of the scale rather than at
   the center. Lehmann's (and Kuznecov's Die morphologische
   Klassifikation ..., 15) discussion of Finck revolves about the
   concept of "load," Lehmann citing as examples of differing
   loads Turkish, which expresses a sentence of two components
   ('he comes') in one word; Chinese in two; and English in three
   ('he is coming'). This should not be construed as indicating
   that English has a lighter load than Chinese, however. The
   base form of the comparison is, after all, the two word
   construction he comes, and there are such forms as come!
4 The use of the terms "root" and "stem" usually implies that
   a bound root is a stem; cf. Eugene A. Nida, Morphology: The
   Descriptive Analysis of Words (2d ed.; Ann Arbor: University
   of Michigan Press, 1949), pp. 82-83. Semitic roots are
   habitually bound, and Finck's terminology might therefore be
   confusing. The real distinction to be made here is not free
   versus bound, but invariant versus variant.
5 Holgar Pedersen, The Discovery of Language: Linguistic Study
   in the Nineteenth Century, trans. John Webster Spargo (Bloomington: Indiana University Press, 1962), p. 125.
6 Under the title of Die Klassifikation der Sprachen.
7 Franz Nikolaus Finck, Die Haupttypen des Sprachbaus (1st ed.;
   Leipzig, 1909).
8 Marr and his Japhetic theory exercised an abnormally great
   influence on Russian linguistic thinking until long after his
   death. Although attacked as early as 1932 by Petr Savvich

Kuznecov, Marr's theories were not laid to rest until he was repudiated by Stalin himself in the Pravda articles of June 20, June 29, and July 22 of 1950.

9 N. J. Marr, "Jafetičeskij Kavkaz i tretij ètničeskij èlement v sozidanii sredizemnomorskoj kul'tury," Izbrannye raboty (Leningrad, 1933-1937), I, p. 98, cited by Lawrence L. Thomas, The Linguistic Theories ..., 118.

10 Edward Sapir, Language: An Introduction to the Study of Speech (New York: Harcourt, Brace & World, Inc., 1921).

11 Ibid., p. 144.

12 Ibid., p. 101. The examples are mine.

13 The distinction between Sapir's Class III and Class IV is not clear-cut. For the purposes of illustration, however, the change from farmer to farmers requires a change in the accompanying verb from sees to see, and therefore transcends the root to which it is applied. Joseph H. Greenberg, "A Quantitative Approach to the Morphological Typology of Language," IJAL, XXVI, No. 3 (1960), p. 183, gives German gender (e.g. d-er Bauer) as a concrete relational concept on the grounds that it indicates nominative singular, masculine. This is open to objection on two grounds: first, it would appear that case, number, and gender are more properly considered syntactic concepts and therefore Class IV; second, d-er can just as readily indicate genitive plural when applied to Bäcker, in which case sentence order--clearly a Class IV concept--is the determining factor.

14 Despite this statement on p. 101 of Language, Sapir indicates a blank under Colum IV in his table on p. 143 of the same book (reproduced on pp. 30-31 infra).

15 Edward Sapir, Language, p. 138.

16 Ibid., pp. 61 and 126.

17 Ibid., p. 132.

18 Ibid., footnote.

19 Ibid., p. 140.

20 But see p. 132, ibid., which designates "symbolic fusion" as "symbolism".

21 Since the total number of combinations of n elements is 2^n-1:

	II	III	IV	Total number of combinations
A	–	–	a,b,c,d	15
B	b,c,d	–	a,b,c,d	7 x 15 = 105
C	–	b,c,d	a,b,c,d	7 x 15 = 105
D	b,c,d	b,c,d	a,b,c,d	7 x 7 x 15 = 735
				960

22 Edward Sapir, Language, p. 127.

23 Ibid., p. 128.
24 Ibid., p. 140.
25 Using the total number of combinations previously computed
    for A, B, C, D and II, III, and IV, we have:

A	analytic only	15 x 1 =	15
B	analytic, synthetic, or polysynthetic	105 x 3 =	315
C	analytic	105 x 1 =	105
	(sometimes synthetic, rarely polysynthetic)	(105 x 2 =	210)
D	analytic, synthetic, or polysynthetic	735 x 3 =	2,205
			(2,870)

26 Edward Sapir, Language, pp. 142-143.
27 Read at the annual meeting of the Linguistic Society of
    America at Philadelphia in December of 1949 and in a talk
    given before the Linguistic Circle of New York at Columbia
    University in January of 1950.
28 In the Festschrift for Wilson D. Wallis, Method and Perspec-
    tive in Anthropology: Papers in Honor of Wilson D. Wallis,
    ed. Robert F. Spencer (Minneapolis: University of Minnesota
    Press, 1954).
29 Joseph H. Greenberg, "A Quantitative Approach to the Mor-
    phological Typology of Language," International Journal of
    American Linguistics, XXVI, No. 3 (1960), pp. 192-220.
30 The construction friend-s (friend plus 'plural'), however, is
    not an agglutinative construction, since the English plural
    morpheme is not automatic.
31 Composition, oddly enough, was never considered separately
    by Sapir as part of his final analytical scale. He does discuss
    the process at length, however, on pp. 65-67 of Language.
32 Joseph H. Greenberg, IJAL, XXVI, No. 3, p. 191.
33 Ibid.
34 Ibid., p. 187.
35 Ibid.
36 Ibid.
37 Ibid.
38 Ibid., p. 193.
39 Ibid., p. 194.
40 André Martinet, A Functional View of Language, p. 39.
41 Ibid., footnote, p. 67. The criticism is superficial, for
    there are extensive differences between the two in method,
    material, and interpretation.
42 Ibid., p. 98.
43 Ibid., p. 97.
44 Martinet uses the term "moneme."
45 Supra, p. 6.

EXAMPLE	F. Schlegel 1808	A. Schlegel 1818	W.v. Humboldt 1822	Bopp 1833	Schleicher 1848
Chinese	Affixing	Without grammatical structure	Isolating	Mono-syllabic roots without grammar	Mono-syllabic
Indo-Chinese					
Bantu		Affixing	Agglutin-ative	Roots capable of composition	Agglutin-ative *analytic
Polynesian					
Turkish					
Amerindian			Incorpo-rating		*synthetic
French	Flexional	Inflexional *analytic	Flexional		Flexional *analytic
Georgian					
Semitic		*synthetic		Disyllabic roots with three con-sonants	*synthetic

Steinthal 1850	Müller 1880	Misteli 1893	Finck 1909	Sapir 1921	EXAMPLE
*form-collocating		Without words	Isolating	Simple pure -relational	
	Radical	*root-isolating	*root-isolating	*analytic	Chinese
*formless-collocating		*stem-isolating	*stem-isolating		Indo-Chinese
*form-derivative by juxta-position			Combining, but not inflected	Simple mixed -relational	
				*synthetic	Bantu
*formless-derivative by prefixes	Termin-ational	*juxta-posing	*juxta-posing	Complex pure -relational *analytic	Polynesian
*formless-derivative by suffixes		With apparent words	*subordin-ating	*synthetic	Turkish
*formless-derivative by incorpo-ration		With sentence words	*incorpo-rating	*incorpo-rating	Amerindian
				Complex mixed -relational *polysynthetic	
			Inflected		
*formless-derivative by "real" suffix	Inflec-tional	With real words	*stem-inflected	*analytic	French
			*group-inflected		Georgian
*form-derivative by inner flexion			*root-inflected	*synthetic	Semitic

BIBLIOGRAPHY

BOOKS

Bopp, Franz. A Comparative Grammar of the Sanskrit, Zend, Greek, Latin, Lithuanian, Gothic, German, and Sclavonic Languages. Trans. Edward B. Eastwick. 3 vols. 3rd ed. London: Williams and Norgate, 1862.

Finck, Franz Nikolaus. Die Haupttypen des Sprachbaus. 3rd ed. Berlin: B. G. Teubner, 1936.

Greenberg, Joseph H. Essays in Linguistics. Chicago: University of Chicago Press, 1957.

Humboldt, Wilhelm von. Wilhelm von Humboldt--Werke. Ed. Andreas Flitner and Klaus Giel. Vol. III. Stuttgart: J. G. Cotta'sche Buchhandlung, 1963.

Jakobson, Roman, Fant, C. Gunnar M., and Halle, Morris. Preliminaries to Speech Analysis: The Distinctive Features and Their Correlates. Cambridge: The MIT Press, 1961.

Jespersen, Otto. Language: Its Nature, Development and Origin. New York: Henry Holt and Company, 1925.

Kuznecov, P. S. Die morphologische Klassifikation der Sprachen. Trans. K. A. Paffen. 2d ed. Halle: VEB Max Niemeyer Verlag, 1960.

Lehmann, Winfred P. Historical Linguistics. New York: Holt, Rinehart and Winston, 1963.

Martinet, André. A Functional View of Language. Oxford: Oxford University Press, 1962.

Müller, F. Max. Lectures on the Science of Language. 2 vols. 6th ed. London: Longmans, Green, and Co., 1880.

Nida, Eugene A. Morphology: The Descriptive Analysis of Words. 2d ed. Ann Arbor: University of Michigan Press, 1949.

Pedersen, Holgar. The Discovery of Language: Linguistic Study in the Nineteenth Century. Trans. John Webster Spargo. Bloomington: Indiana University Press, 1962.

Sapir, Edward. Language: An Introduction to the Study of Speech. New York: Harcourt, Brace & World, Inc., 1921.

Schlegel, August Wilhelm von. Observations sur la langue et la littérature provençales. Paris: Librairie grecque-latine-allemande, 1818.

Schlegel, Karl Wilhelm Friedrich von. Ueber die Sprache und Weisheit der Indier. Heidelberg: Mohr und Zimmer, 1808.

Schleicher, August. A Compendium of the Comparative Grammar of the Indo-European, Sanskrit, Greek and Latin Languages. Trans. from Part I of the 3rd German ed. (1861) by Herbert Bendall. London: Trübner and Company, 1874.

————. Die Sprachen Europas in systematischer Uebersicht. Bonn: H. B. König, 1850.

————. Zur vergleichenden Sprachengeschichte. Bonn: H. B. König, 1848.

Schmidt, Fr. Wilhelm. Die Sprachfamilien und Sprachenkreise der Erde. Heidelberg: Carl Winters Universitätsbuchhandlung, 1926.

Steinthal, Heymann. Die Classifikation der Sprachen, dargestellt als die Entwicklung der Sprachidee. Berlin: Dümmler, 1850.

————. Charakteristik der hauptsächlichisten Typen des Sprachbaues. Berlin: Dümmler, 1860.

Thomas, Lawrence L. The Linguistic Theories of N. Ja. Marr. University of California Publications in Linguistics. Vol. 14. Berkeley: University of California Press, 1957.

Waterman, John T. Perspectives in Linguistics. Chicago: The University of Chicago Press, 1963.

Whitney, William Dwight. Language and the Study of Language: Twelve Lectures on the Principles of Linguistic Science. New York: Charles Scribner & Co., 1870.

Whorf, Benjamin Lee. Collected Papers on Metalinguistics. Washington: Foreign Service Institute, 1952.

ARTICLES

Greenberg, Joseph H. "The Nature and Uses of Linguistic
Typologies," International Journal of American Linguistics,
Vol. 23, No. 2 (1957), pp. 68-77.
————. "A Quantitative Approach to the Morphological
Typology of Language," International Journal of American
Linguistics, Vol. 26, No. 3 (1960), pp. 178-194.
Hartmann, Peter. "Zur Erforschung von Sprachtypen: Methoden
und Anwendungen," II. Fachtagung für indogermanische und
allgemeine Sprachwissenschaft. Innsbrucker Beiträge zur
Kulturwissenschaft, Sonderheft 15. Innsbruck: Sprach-
wissenschaftliches Institut der Leopold-Franzens-Universität
Innsbruck, 1962, pp. 31-55.
Hockett, Charles F. "A Manual of Phonology," International
Journal of American Linguistics, Vol. 21, No. 4, Part 1,
1955.
Hymes, Dell H. "On Typology of Cognitive Styles in Language,"
Anthropological Linguistics, Vol. 3, No. 1 (1961), pp. 22-54.
Jakobson, Roman et al. "What Can Typological Studies Contrib-
ute to Historical Comparative Linguistics?" Proceedings of
the Eighth International Congress of Linguists. Oslo: Oslo
University Press, 1958, pp. 17-35.
Jespersen, Otto. "The Classification of Languages," The
Selected Writings of Otto Jespersen. London: George Allen
& Unwin Ltd., 1960, pp. 693-704.
Kroeber, A. L. "On Typological Indices I: Ranking of Languages,"
International Journal of American Linguistics, Vol. 26, No. 3
(1960), pp. 171-177.
Meillet, Antoine. "Introduction à la Classification des Langues,"
Linguistique Historique et Linguistique Générale. Paris:
Champion, 1948, pp. 53-69 of appendix.
Menzerath, Paul. "Typology of Languages," Journal of the
Acoustical Society of America, Vol. 22 (1950), pp. 698-701.
Odendal, F. F. "Limitations of Morphological Processes: A
Note," Lingua, Vol. 12 (1963), pp. 220-225.
Pierce, Joe E. "Possible Electronic Computation of Typological
Indices for Linguistic Structures," International Journal of
American Linguistics, Vol. 28, No. 4 (1962), pp. 215-226.
Stewart, William A. "An Outline of Linguistic Typology for
Describing Multilingualism," Study of the Role of Second
Languages in Asia, Africa, and Latin America. Washington:
Center for Applied Linguistics of the Modern Language

Association of America, 1962, pp. 15-25.

Trubetzkoy, Nikolas S. "Zur allgemeinen Theorie der phono-logischen Vokalsysteme," Travaux du Cercle Linguistique de Prague, Vol. I (1929), pp. 39-67.

————. "Die phonologischen Systeme," Travaux du Cercle Linguistique de Prague, Vol. IV (1931), pp. 96-116.

Uhlenbeck, E. M. "Limitations of Morphological Processes: Some Preliminary Remarks," Lingua, Vol. 11 (1962), pp. 426-432.

Ullmann, Stephen. "Descriptive Semantics and Linguistic Typology," Word, Vol. 9, No. 3 (1953), pp. 225-240.

Voegelin, C. F. "On Developing New Typologies and Revising Old Ones," Southwestern Journal of Anthropology, Vol. 11 (1955), pp. 355-360.

————. "Subsystems within Systems in Cultural and Linguistic Typologies," For Roman Jakobson. The Hague: 1956, pp. 592-599.

————. "Methods for Typologizing Directly and by Distinctive Features (in reference to Uto-Aztecan and Kiowa-Tanoan vowel systems)," Lingua, XI (1962), pp. 469-487.

————, and Yegerlehner, John. "The Scope of Whole System ('Distinctive Feature') and Subsystem Typologies," Word, Vol. 12 (1956), pp. 198-205.

Wells, Rulon. "Archiving and Language Typology," International Journal of American Linguistics, Vol. 20, No. 2 (1954), pp. 101-107.

Wolff, Hans. "Sub-system Typologies and Area Linguistics," Anthropological Linguistics, Vol. 1, No. 7 (1959).

MONOGRAPH SERIES ON LANGUAGES AND LINGUISTICS

No. 1 (2nd RTM) Meeting the Government's Needs in Languages, Linguistic Theory and Pedagogical Application, The Language Laboratory. Edited by John de Francis, September 1951.

No. 2 (3rd RTM) Meeting America's Needs in Languages, The Language Laboratory, Linguistic Science and Pedagogical Application. Edited by Salvatore Castiglione, September 1952.

No. 3 The Vowel Phonemes of Meigret, by George Raymond Shipman, April 1953.

No. 4 (4th RTM) Problems of Testing in Language Instruction, Technical Aids in Language Teaching and Research, Linguistics and the Humanities. Edited by A. A. Hill, September 1953.

No. 5 Audio-Visual Aids in Language Teaching, by Ruth Hirsch, March 1954.

No. 6 Applied Linguistics in Language Teaching. Edited by Ernest Pulgram, July 1954.

No. 7 (5th RTM) Bilingualism and Mixed Languages, The Spectrographic Analysis of Speech, Language and Culture. Edited by Hugo Mueller, September 1954.

No. 8 (6th RTM) Applied Linguistics and the Preparation of Teaching Materials, Problems of Translation, Meaning and Language Structure. Edited by Ruth Hirsch Weinstein, September 1955.

No. 9 (7th RTM) Approaches to Syntax, The Teaching of English as a Foreign Language, Perspectives of Linguistic Science. Edited by Paul L. Garvin, December 1957.

No. 10 (8th RTM) Research in Machine Translation. Edited by Leon Dostert, December 1957.

No. 11 (9th RTM) African Studies, Cultural Anthropology, Anthropology and Linguistics. Edited by William M. Austin.

No. 12 (10th RTM) African Studies, The Teaching of Arabic, Trends in Modern Linguistic Theory. Edited by Richard S. Harrell, 1959.

No. 13 (11th RTM) Language and Meaning, Linguistics and Literature, Culture and Language Teaching. Edited by Bernard Choseed and Allene Guss, April 1960.

No. 14 (12th RTM) General Semantics, Psycho-linguistics, Lexicography. Edited by Michael Zarechnak and Allene Guss, April 1961.

No. 15 (13th RTM) Bilingualism, Transformation Theory, National Languages and Diglossia. Edited by Elisabeth D. Woodworth, Robert J. Di Pietro and Allene Guss, April 1962.

No. 16 (14th RTM) Linguistics and Philosophy, Modern Approaches to Grammatical Analysis, Linguistics and the Learning Processes. Edited by Robert J. Di Pietro, April 1963.

No. 17 (15th RTM) Current Research in Syntax Outside the United States, Achievement in Linguistic Theory, Subject-Matter Relations Between Linguistics and Other Disciplines. Edited by C. I. J. M. Stuart, June 1964.

No. 18 (16th RTM) Approaches to Linguistic Analysis, Language and Society Teaching Language Skills. Edited by Charles W. Kreidler, 1965.

No. 19 (17th RTM) Problems in Semantics, History of Linguistics, Linguistics and English. Edited by Francis P. Dinneen, S.J., 1966.